SHAPED BY SCRIPTURE

For We Are God's Handiwork

EPHESIANS

DOUG WARD

10 9 8 7 6 5 4 3 2 1

Contents

THE *SHAPED BY SCRIPTURE* SERIES

The first step of an organized study of the Bible is the selection of a biblical book, which is not always an easy task. Often people pick a book they are already familiar with, books they think will be easy to understand, or books that, according to popular opinion, seem to have more relevance to Christians today than other books of the Bible. However, it is important to recognize the truth that God's Word is not limited to just a few books. All the biblical books, both individually and collectively, communicate God's Word to us. As Paul affirms in 2 Timothy 3:16, "All Scripture is God-breathed and is useful for teaching, rebuking, correcting and training in righteousness." We interpret the term "God-breathed" to mean inspired by God. If Christians are going to take 2 Timothy 3:16 seriously, then we should all set the goal of encountering God's Word as communicated through all sixty-six books of the Bible. New Christians or those with little to no prior knowledge of the Bible might find it best to start with a New Testament book like 1 John, James, or the Gospel of John.

By purchasing this volume, you have chosen to study the book of Ephesians, which reveals much about our relationship with God and others as well as our new life in Christ. The goal of this series is to illustrate an appropriate method of studying the Bible. Since Ephesians is a short, six-chapter book, it is a perfect size for in-depth Bible study.

How This Study Works

This Bible study is intended for a period of seven weeks. We have chosen a specific passage for each week's study. This study can be done individually or with a small group.

For individual study, we recommend a five-day study each week, following the guidelines given below:

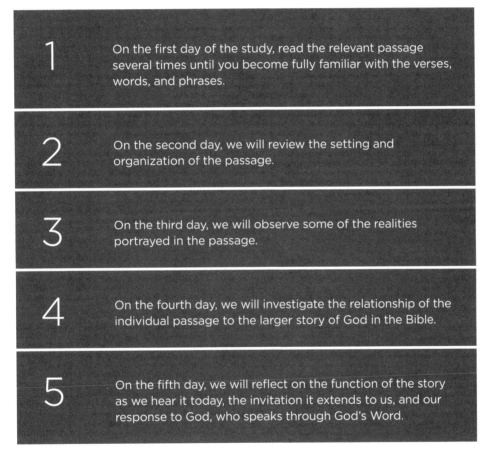

1   On the first day of the study, read the relevant passage several times until you become fully familiar with the verses, words, and phrases.

2   On the second day, we will review the setting and organization of the passage.

3   On the third day, we will observe some of the realities portrayed in the passage.

4   On the fourth day, we will investigate the relationship of the individual passage to the larger story of God in the Bible.

5   On the fifth day, we will reflect on the function of the story as we hear it today, the invitation it extends to us, and our response to God, who speaks through God's Word.

If this Bible study is done as a group activity, we recommend that members of the group meet together on the sixth day to share and discuss what they have learned from God's Word and how it has transformed their lives.

You may want to have a study Bible to give you additional insights as we work through the book of Ephesians. Other helpful resources are *Discovering the New Testament* and *Ephesians/ Colossians/Philemon: A Commentary in the Wesleyan Tradition*, available from The Foundry Publishing.

Literary Forms in the Bible

There are several literary forms represented throughout the Bible. The divinely inspired writers used various techniques to communicate God's Word to their ancient audiences. The major literary forms (also known as genres) of the Bible are:

- narratives

- laws

- history

- Wisdom literature (in the form of dialogues and proverbial statements)

- poetry (consisting of poems of praise, lament, trust in God, and more)

- prophecy

- discourses

- parables

- miracle stories

- letters (also known as epistles)

- exhortations

- apocalyptic writings

Within each of these forms, one may find subgenres. Each volume in the *Shaped by Scripture* series will briefly overview the genres found in the book of the Bible that is the subject of that study.

When biblical writers utilized a particular literary form, they intended for it to have a specific effect on their audience. This concept can be understood by examining genres that are familiar to us in our contemporary setting. For example, novels that are comedies inspire good and happy feelings in their readers; tragedies, on the other hand, are meant to induce sorrow. What is true of the intended effect of literary forms in contemporary literature is also true of literary forms found in the Bible.

THE BOOK OF EPHESIANS

The message of the biblical books, though it originates with God, comes to us through individuals whom God inspired to communicate his word to humanity. They fulfilled their task by utilizing their literary skill as speakers and writers of God's message. This message came to these individuals in particular circumstances in the history of God's people—the Israelites in the Old Testament period, and the Christian church in the first century AD. In addition, biblical books communicate certain clearly developed understandings about God, humanity, sin, judgment, salvation, human hope, and more. Bible studies should be done with an awareness of the theological themes in a particular book. So, prior to our engagement with the actual text of Ephesians, we will briefly summarize what we know about the book in general, the authorship of Ephesians, literary forms found in the book, the historical setting of the book and that of its writing, and its major theological themes.

The Pauline Epistles

The book of Ephesians is part of a collection of thirteen New Testament letters attributed to the apostle Paul. There are epistles that fall in this category whose authorship is debated or unknown (Ephesians is one of those), but tradition still attributes them to Paul. Included in the list of Pauline epistles are Romans, 1 & 2 Corinthians, Galatians, Ephesians, Philippians, Colossians, 1 & 2 Thessalonians, 1 & 2 Timothy, Titus, and Philemon. Of these, the first nine are written to church congregations while the last four are known as pastoral epistles because, with the exception of Philemon, they are written to individuals who lead churches or groups of churches. Sometimes Hebrews is included in the list of Pauline epistles and sometimes it isn't, since Hebrews has been attributed to Paul in the past but the current consensus is that the author is unknown or anonymous. Epistles that aren't attributed to Paul belong to a category known as the general epistles.

One aspect that sets apart Paul's letters from other New Testament books is his tender, pastoral desire for a holy and faithful church. Paul makes clear in all of his letters both his love for Christ and his love for the congregations he has helped to plant and pastor. One of Paul's overarching ministry goals is to encourage all believers—whether Jewish Christians or Greek/gentile Christians—to remain united in their participation in the mission of God, and to have right hearts before God and with each other. Paul strongly believed that a mature and developed inward faith and relationship with

Jesus would lead all Christians into living out their faith in an outward manner that would bless the world and be a faithful representation of the church and an enduring witness to God.

Who Wrote Ephesians?

Ephesians is one of the New Testament letters where the identity of the author is in some dispute. Traditionally, the author of Ephesians has been considered to be Paul. In recent decades scholars have identified reasons to doubt Pauline authorship, noting some differences in the words and style of writing used, but there is also good reason to continue considering Paul the author. In Ephesians the divide between Jews and gentiles is still front and center. Readers of Ephesians can note how often the author slips between references to "you" and references to "we" in the first two chapters. Internal evidence shows the "we" group to be the Jews—"the first to hope in Christ." This evidence would place the writing of Ephesians before the destruction of Jerusalem and the Jewish wing of the fledgling church that happened in AD 70. Any letter written after 70, therefore, would be to a church that is overwhelmingly gentile. We understand Paul to have still been alive and active in ministry before 70, so it is difficult to envision a letter written by someone else in his name before his death. Since there is no compelling reason to overturn the traditional claim that Paul was the author and since it will have no bearing on our study here, we will move forward with the understanding that Paul is the author.

Literary Form

Ephesians is one of the many books in the New Testament that was written as a letter. It is only slightly different in the fact that it is a circular letter, which means it was meant to be distributed among many churches instead of directed toward one specific church. Circular letters were often read aloud in a congregation before being passed on to the next church.

Ancient letters followed a particular form, and Ephesians does as well. Ancient letters started with a salutation, which simply consists of naming the sender, the audience, and a greeting. Most letters then followed with a thanksgiving section, where the author listed all the reasons they were thankful for the addressee(s). Then followed the main body, or the particular issue that the letter addresses. The main body contained the reason for the letter and all of the discussion about a particular issue. The next part of an ancient letter is called the paraenesis, or practical instructions. The best way to describe this section would be to say that after the author has laid out the main argument, the author then writes how the audience should respond. The letter usually closed with a very short section containing final greetings and perhaps instructions for the one who delivered the letter or an appeal to a particular person within the larger group addressed.

It is important to remember when we read one of Paul's letters that we are reading someone's mail. While we can learn a great deal from these letters that are the inspired Word of God, we need to remember that we are only reading half of a correspondence. We do not know with certainty the particularities of the situation or the details of the previous communication that Paul is answering. The best we can do is try to recreate the situation by looking closely at what we have, and by studying the time and place of these letters in order to gain an understanding of the way they were intended to be read originally. Once we ascertain an original purpose, we may then proceed to determine what meaning these important scriptures might have for us today.

Date

If we consider Ephesians to be Pauline, that places the letter within a limited time frame. Since Paul died in the early to mid 60s, depending on which church tradition is accurate, Ephesians must have been written before this time. Internal evidence in this letter gives us additional guidance about the date. Paul mentions that he is "in chains." While a shorter prison stay in Ephesus is possible, most people place Paul's letter writing sometime during his long prison stays in either Caesarea or Rome. Paul was in prison in Caesarea from roughly AD 58–60, and under house arrest in Rome from 60–62. This is the period of time that also produced Colossians, Philippians, and Philemon. We might also note how similar Ephesians is to Colossians. This similarity has caused some to claim that Ephesians is a later work that copied liberally from Colossians. A more plausible explanation is to see two similar works, where Colossians is addressed to a specific church while Ephesians is meant to be passed around among many churches. Both of these letters fit comfortably into the time frame of Paul's imprisonment.

Entering the Story

Paul lived a tumultuous life. While it might be safe to say that is the type of life he wanted to live, it was not the life he originally planned. Everything started like he had foreseen. He was zealous and driven and wanted to ascend to the highest levels of Jewish life. He ascended quickly through the ranks of Jewish leadership and had been entrusted with the task of ensuring that the practice of Judaism was both correct and doctrinally pure. He pursued this task with vigor, right up until the afternoon when he was on his way to Damascus and had his encounter with Jesus Christ. On an afternoon when Paul least expected it, everything changed.

The next 12–15 years were the hardest on Paul. He was prepared for leadership and loved the responsibility and the intensity of the intellectual battle. Paul was prepared for hard times, but he was not prepared for the difficulty of being relegated to the sidelines. In the space of a few weeks Paul went from Jewish leader to an utterly forgotten man. Suddenly, Paul was a man without a constituency. He was alone in the world. His experience left him both unwilling and unfit to serve in Jewish leadership anymore, and there were no Christian churches that trusted him. After all, how do you get people to trust you when you spent the previous years making life difficult for them? Paul yearned to serve the Jesus he met on the road to Damascus, but the early believers wanted nothing to do with him.

No longer welcome in Jerusalem, Paul found a new home in and around Antioch. We do not know exactly what filled these years, but Paul was slowly making himself part of the church there and making sense of what happened to him on that dusty road. He had spent his entire life following the law in a way that he described as faultless (Phil. 3:6), yet somehow he had still found himself at odds with God. As he returned to his beloved Hebrew Scriptures, he found some comforting and familiar words, such as "the righteous person will live by his faithfulness" (Hab. 2:4) and the promise that in the last days God would "pour out [his] Spirit on all people" (Joel 2:28). These ancient words became a new center of thought for Paul, a life that revolved around faith, and a daily walk with the Spirit.

10

After more than a decade of solitary existence, the church in Antioch gave Paul a new task — go and make disciples just as Jesus had instructed. Armed with his customary zeal and his new understanding of what constituted God's people, Paul took to his new task with enthusiasm. He traveled throughout the Roman Empire, telling anyone who would listen that they could be a part of God's family. He spent much of his time arguing his new understanding to his own people, the Jews, but he was not making much progress. Surprisingly, his message was received warmly and enthusiastically by gentiles. Finally, Paul had a people once again. It was not easy. There were many struggles along the way. There were evictions, arrests, imprisonments, and beatings to be endured, but Paul was ready for the battle. In some ways the battle was better than his silent, solitary years. In the worst of the trials, he had always been renewed by the constant presence of the Holy Spirit and the thought that his life would not be in vain after all.

There was one other struggle that followed Paul wherever he traveled. Once Paul left his new churches, he left behind a new mix of Jewish and gentile believers. The Jewish believers kept their traditional practices and ceremonies, but these new gentile believers felt no obligation to assume Jewish practices. When some Jewish believers tried to compel the gentiles to adopt the Jewish regulations, Paul responded in places like Galatia and told his churches no. Do not force the gentiles to become Jews in order to follow Christ, Paul instructed. This would be the standard Pauline instruction for all of his churches.

Now Paul was in the latter years of his life. He was under house arrest in Rome, and his future was uncertain. He did not know whether he would be released or face death at the hands of Caesar. While under house arrest, Paul could entertain visitors and talk with them; he just could not leave. While in Rome, Paul heard news from his churches. Many of these were churches that Paul founded himself or visited numerous times. However, there were other churches that Paul did not start. It seemed some of his converts were starting churches themselves. Even though these churches did not know Paul personally, they had heard of his life and his reputation as an encourager. Across the miles Paul felt a connection to these people. He wanted to help these new churches start on solid ground, so he penned a letter from Rome that he hoped would be passed around from church to church. This is the letter we know as Ephesians.

Historical Context

As Paul wrote this letter, the church was still very young. The center of the church still existed in Jerusalem under the leadership of James and largely consisted of Jewish believers. Though they believed in Christ, they took their Jewish heritage seriously, and that heritage served as an obstacle in their relationship with these gentiles. Paul's relationship with the church in Jerusalem was strained at best, and his imprisonment in Rome was the distant result of his arrest in Jerusalem—an arrest that was driven by the Jewish believers' continued distrust of Paul.

This strained relationship drove Paul to his missionary journeys around the Roman Empire. The conflict with these Jewish believers was not Paul's only issue in the early church. After emphasizing freedom from the law for the gentile believers, some gentiles took that freedom to an extreme. We can read about the harmful extremes that some believers exemplified in Paul's letter to the Corinthians. Even in some early churches, there was disdain toward not only the Jewish regulations but also most moral guidelines and restrictions. This caused Paul to wage a war on two fronts. On one side were the Jews who wished to impose their legal requirements on the gentiles, and on the other side were gentiles who wished to distance themselves from their Jewish fellow believers.

Hanging over every aspect of first-century life was the reality of the Roman Empire and, if Paul was writing from prison, the heavy-handed specter of Nero. It is hard to overemphasize how prevalent the presence of Nero would have been in every corner of the empire. As with most caesars, Nero would have desired a lack of conflict in every part of the empire. Any reported unrest would risk a sharp response with all of the power and might that only Rome could possess. If any squabble between the

Jews and gentiles made the authorities notice, then the believers could be subject to imprisonment or death. The early Christians had seen enough prison and death, and Paul wanted to avoid further unnecessary suffering.

Even though the early church was fairly powerless politically, Paul still envisioned a grand role for the church to play. The church was at the center of a drama that transcended any local area but included the greater Roman Empire and even unseen forces. When the church overcomes the things that divide us, we announce to the world that Jesus is Lord and that Caesar is not. We even announce to the forces that stand against us that their influence is waning *because* Jesus is Lord. Mere words will never accomplish this proclamation, but the lives of his people will.

In the comfort of our modern world we tend to believe that "Jesus is Lord" is merely a slogan we use in worship. It is a proclamation we make on Sunday. In AD 62, however, the terms "Lord" and "Son of God" were terms that caesars used to describe themselves. The power they proclaimed for themselves was more than political; it was all-encompassing. When the early believers proclaimed that Jesus was the Son of God, it was more than a church saying. It was a political statement that the political powers noticed. Unless your life is on the line, that is easy to forget.

Context of the Letter

As Paul lingered under house arrest, all of his missionary work among the gentiles hung in the balance. Would these young churches survive, or would Christianity drift back into an intra-Jewish phenomenon? Thankfully, new churches were starting, and while Paul did not personally know these churches, he felt a certain responsibility for their well-being. One of the benefits of his imprisonment in Rome was that Paul had the time to collect his thoughts and write. Many have noticed the similarities between Ephesians and Colossians, and there are definitely common themes between these letters. Imprisoned Paul wrote this circular letter and sent it with Tychicus, along with his letter to the Colossians. While Colossians was meant for a specific church, Ephesians reached a larger audience.

Many themes in Ephesians were crafted especially for the gentile part of the church. Paul wanted to remind them that, while they were not subject to the Jewish laws, they had a certain responsibility to appreciate what was passed down to them. The salvation and new life they enjoyed did not come to them alone but through the Jewish wing of the church. Therefore, they had a responsibility to live in unity with their Jewish brothers and sisters.

In the Roman Empire, as we do today, believers had a careful responsibility to live in unity with one another, including people very different from themselves. How can we stand as a light to our world if we cannot overcome the ethnic and cultural differences that exist in the world? If we cannot overcome these petty divisions why would anyone listen to our message? In pursuit of these ends, Ephesians is a letter filled with uplifting prayers not only for unity but also for all believers to know the greatness of the love of God. Knowing this love is more than an academic pursuit; it is a vital reality if the church is to proclaim its message.

This unity is not only a collective experience between Jew and gentile, but it is also expressed in individual relationships. Ephesians also outlines guidance for husbands/ wives, parents/children, and slaves/masters. Paul gave these instructions in what is known as a household code from 5:21 to 6:9. These codes were well known in the ancient world, and many Greek writers produced a list of household instructions like Paul's example in chapters 5 and 6. In the Greek world these codes were always written to the male head of the household and told the male leaders how to rule over their household and manage their affairs. All other relationships in the house were told how to behave toward the head of the household. No Greek writer would directly address women or the servants in the household. Such communications were beneath the dignity of the writer. When we come to this section in chapter 5, we need to remember that these commands were written in that culture and reflected certain realities in the Greco-Roman world. We must read in light of those sensibilities before trying to ascertain the meaning for us today.

What is important for the audience of this letter is still important today. We must have unity in Christ. While our divide is no longer along Jewish and gentile lines, our divisions today are just as real and the need for healing just as great. The world was watching in Asia Minor in the first century, and it is still watching. Let the words of this letter inform your world just as it did theirs.

Major Theological Themes

Ephesians is primarily concerned with the unity of believers, but it is rich with other theological themes we can explore along the way.

 Christ has defeated the forces that stand against believers through his death and resurrection. Even more importantly, Christ raises us to be united with him..

 Everything that God has done has pointed to this moment. The calling of the Jewish people and the redeeming work of Christ have been done so that the gentiles—the entire world—would be included in the family of God.

 The church is called to overcome its ethnic and social divisions.

 The church is meant to mediate the power and presence of God to the world through Christ.

Believers are active participants in the new life Christ provides. We are called to purposefully practice a new way of life and abandon our old habits.

 The most important place believers can demonstrate our new way of life is within our family relationships.

 Even though Paul started his life as a zealous Jew, God had a different purpose for Paul. Paul's life and his current imprisonment are for the benefit of the gentiles. Paul is someone they can trust.

 God is the one who equips believers with what we need to withstand and fight against the forces of evil we will encounter in the world.

15

EPHESIANS 1

Paul understood that the future viability of the church rested on whether it would be a unified body of believers. The question that Paul faced was how to get the Jewish believers to accept these new gentiles, and how to convince the gentiles to appreciate the Jews. It would not be an easy task. Paul takes these opening words in Ephesians and guides gentile readers on a history lesson of God's work with the Jews.

Paul wants to convince the readers that the Jews are not children of God by their own effort; rather, they were chosen by God, but not for their own sake. God chose them to be a priestly nation that would bring blessing to the whole world. This purpose becomes most clearly evident in the person of Jesus. Non-Jews gained direct access to God because of Christ. Paul wants his gentile readers to know they are fully included in God's family, but he also wants them to appreciate that they are part of a family that started with the Jews.

WEEK 1, DAY 1

Absorb the passage in Ephesians 1 by reading it aloud several times until you become familiar with its verses, words, and phrases.

WEEK 1, DAY 2

EPHESIANS 1

The Setting

In chapter 3 Paul explicitly states that he is in chains, so scholars believe that this letter was written during his confinement in Rome. Paul was not in a prison, but he was under guard, not free to come and go as he pleased. It would be similar to a type of house arrest. For two years Paul was in Rome awaiting his chance to present his case before Caesar, which was his right as a Roman citizen.

The arrest that led to this imprisonment happened years before, when Paul was in Jerusalem. The mistrust from years earlier had not gone away, and Paul had been the focus of unrest because he was suspected of appeasing gentiles. After all of his journeys and all of his work, the Jews and gentiles were still suspicious of each other, even in the church. As Paul sat quietly in his place of confinement, his mind probably wandered to the churches he started and other churches he did not begin, and he worried about their survival. While he could not visit these churches personally, he decided to write a letter that could be read to them.

The Message

Part of our struggle as modern readers is to correctly determine the intent of the author. Whenever we read one of Paul's letters, we realize that we are only reading half of the conversation. We must do our best to determine the rest of the conversation from clues within the letter. Ephesians is not an exception to this rule. Reading one of Paul's letters is like listening to a phone conversation in our world; we try to understand the context even as we realize there is another person in the overheard conversation that we do not see or hear.

This letter is intended for a number of churches in Asia Minor that are dominated by gentiles. Paul had never seen many of these churches, so we can assume they were started by people in Paul's other churches. Paul wanted to help these new believers appreciate the value and history of their faith. While Paul was grateful for every gentile believer, he also wanted to ensure that these believers appreciated the Jewish roots of their faith. Such an appreciation, Paul believed, would help unite Jew and gentile and develop a unity in the faith as an example for the world.

To discover the message of Ephesians 1, let's divide the chapter into five sections. Below, summarize or paraphrase the general message or theme of each grouping of verses (following the pattern provided for verses 1–2).

1. Ephesians 1:1–2

This is the salutation or customary greeting in an ancient letter.

_____

_____

2. Ephesians 1:3–10

_____

_____

_____

_____

_____

_____

_____

_____

_____

3. Ephesians 1:11–14

_____

_____

_____

_____

_____

_____

_____

4. Ephesians 1:15–19a

_____

_____

_____

_____

_____

_____

_____

_____

_____

_____

_____

_____

_____

_____

_____

5. Ephesians 1:19b–23

_____

_____

_____

_____

_____

_____

_____

_____

_____

_____

_____

_____

_____

_____

WEEK 1, DAY 3

What's Happening in the Passage?

As we read through these passages there are certain ideas and words that were familiar to the original readers but are not as familiar to us. Two thousand years and a vastly different culture obscure some of these ideas from us today. You may encounter some of these words and ideas in your study today. Some of them have been explained in more detail in the **Word Study Notes**. If you want even more detail you can supplement this study with a Bible dictionary or commentary.

1. Ephesians 1:1–2

This is Paul's typical greeting in his letters. Paul always greets his fellow Christians by calling them saints, or designating them as holy. Today we tend to reserve that kind of terminology for only those special people whom we think rise above other believers, but for Paul, holy people—or saints—are simply people who are set apart for the mission of God.

Paul always ends his greetings by wishing his people grace and peace. By extending grace, Paul is wishing them unmerited favor and kindness from God. It is a gentle reminder that we are not deserving of God's grace. He also wishes them peace, which is a grounded settledness, regardless of circumstances, that God alone can provide. It is a fitting and uplifting greeting.

2. Ephesians 1:3–10

This is a passage that introduces us to the word "predestined."[1] As we approach this passage, we must remain grounded in the historical context of Paul and his letter. We might be tempted to start any conversation about predestination with our modern arguments, but Paul lived 1,500 years prior to the Reformation, so we must try to ascertain what Paul meant in his time.

In Asia Minor people were used to hearing the word "mystery" in relation to religious thought, so Paul imported this word into

WORD STUDY NOTES #2

[1] We tend to notice the big words, and in this section the big word is "predestined." Yet we often fail to see the smaller words and the historical context that stands behind the passage. Notice the use of the first- and second-person plural throughout this passage. Each time words like "chosen" and "predestined" are used, it is within the context of the "we" group (first-person plural). Paul identifies that group as the Jews—the first to hope in Christ. Yet this is also the group that is rejecting Christ while the gentiles are accepting Christ. So in Ephesians, the "predestined" are not a limited group of people for whom salvation is selectively possible; the word "predestined" is instead a simple reference to the history of the Jewish people.

his letter. After centuries of rigorous law observance and the memory of his own experience, Paul has reoriented his thinking. Paul starts this letter by guiding the readers through this divine plan that has been made known.

This plan began with the Jews, who were chosen to be adopted into God's family. This process started with the obedience of Abraham, Isaac, and Jacob. Yet this adoption was not accomplished just so the Jews could enjoy special favor. The Jews were chosen so that, at the proper time, all things would be brought to unity, starting with the many times that Jews in the Old Testament were called to be hospitable to strangers and foreigners in their midst, and continuing in the New Testament with the inclusion of gentiles in the plan of God. This is what Paul has spent the previous years fighting for—full acceptance of the gentiles into the church.

3. Ephesians 1:11–14

Paul continues to explain the content of God's plan, and he expands his thoughts about the Jews, yet it is at this point that Paul turns his attention to the gentiles with the words "you also." Now Jew and gentile are united in God's family. After a life dedicated to the performance of the law, a new marker has replaced the law, and it is the Spirit.[1] Paul realizes the gentiles are equal because he has seen the Spirit being poured out on both Jew and gentile, just as Joel 2:28 promised. The Spirit has been given to both Jew and gentile as a guarantee that we are united together in God's kingdom.

Create your own brief summary or description of the reality portrayed in verses 15–19a.

4. Ephesians 1:15–19a[1]

_____

_____

_____

_____

_____

22

5. Ephesians 1:19b–23[1,2,3]

Christians can ask God daily for wisdom, knowing they will not be shamed by God for asking and that God will give the wisdom needed.

WORD STUDY NOTES #5

[1] This passage lifts our awareness beyond our issue and raises our vision to a cosmic level. "Heavenly realms" is shorthand for the place where God lives. Ancient Jewish cosmology saw the world as concentric circles with humanity living on earth, with three (or sometimes seven) levels of heaven. We live in the first, earthly layer, while God occupies the highest level. Paul referred to his own experience on the road to Damascus as being taken to the third heaven in 2 Corinthians 12:2. These words are a cultural way for Paul to say that what happened to him could not be described in a normal way. He had to have been in the presence of God.

[2] Paul reminds Christians that Rome, and every other earthly power, lives far below the power of Christ. These powers combined together and willfully participated in the death of Christ. Earthly powers rendered him guilty, the law was used as a catalyst for his death, and dark forces supported them, but with the resurrection, all of these powers have been soundly defeated. Now Jesus stands above everything for the benefit of the church. Even when things look the darkest, Christ is the head of everything.

[3] Paul is simply acknowledging the reality of earthly forces, political forces, and even evil forces that might stand behind their earthly allies. In a time when Rome and Nero reigned, no one needed convincing that dark and sinister forces were at work. In Asia Minor people feared these powers. The simple message is that, even at their most powerful, these forces pale in comparison to the resurrection of Christ and are never the equal of Christ. In our own world, "the devil made me do it" must never be the excuse for any Christian.

23

Discoveries

Let's summarize our discoveries from Ephesians 1.

1. We have learned that Paul is speaking specifically to Jews and gentiles in different parts of this letter.

2. We know that the Jews were the chosen people, but that chosen status was so that all people may come to know Christ.

3. The indwelling presence of the Holy Spirit is the central sign that God is working in the midst of his people.

4. We see that Paul takes seriously the powers and forces that stand opposed to the church.

5. Even though the church's opposing forces are real, we serve a Christ who has already defeated them. Therefore we can have confidence.

WEEK 1, DAY 4

A Chosen Family and the Story of God

Whenever we read a biblical text, it is important to ask how the particular text we are reading relates to the rest of the Bible. As we have already discussed, Paul's ministry was about overcoming the divisions between Jews and gentiles and spreading the good news to the gentiles. When the gentiles came into the church it created issues, especially for the Jewish believers who had already believed in God for years. However, God working through unexpected people is not a new storyline. There are other places where God moved in unexpected ways and used unexpected people.

Places in Scripture where these themes are notably present include but are not limited to Genesis 25:19–34, Ruth 4, Jonah 3, Luke 7:1–10, and Acts 8:26–40. **In the space given below, write a short summary of each passage, identifying how these stories illustrate the theme of God acting in a manner that others may not have expected.**

Genesis 25:19–34

_____

_____

_____

_____

_____

_____

Ruth 4

_____

_____

_____

_____

_____

_____

_____

If you have a study Bible, it may have references in a margin, a middle column, or footnotes that point to other biblical texts. You may find it helpful in understanding how the whole story of God ties together to look up some of those other scriptures from time to time.

Jonah 3

_____
_____
_____
_____
_____
_____
_____
_____

Luke 7:1–10

_____
_____
_____
_____
_____
_____
_____
_____
_____
_____

Acts 8:26–40

_____
_____
_____
_____
_____
_____
_____
_____
_____
_____

WEEK 1, DAY 5

Ephesians and Our World Today

When we look at the themes of God's chosen family and the riches of Christ in Ephesians 1, they can become the lens through which we see ourselves, our world, and how God works in our world today.

1. Paul calls the believers "holy" or "saints" in his greeting. This is a word we typically use today only for a select few. Do you think God views believers in the way Paul describes?

It is clear that Scripture calls all believers saints because saints are those whom God sets apart

to actively seek after God and to participate in the mission of God in the world. God also looks

at our potential and what we have become in Christ instead of looking at our every weakness.

Following the above example, answer these questions about how we can understand ourselves, our world, and God's action in our world today.

2. If there were a pre-chosen few who were the only ones to be redeemed, how would that make you feel?

27

_____

_____

_____

_____

3. If everyone is the focus of God's salvation, how should that change our behavior?

_____

_____

_____

_____

4. In Paul's first prayer in Ephesians, he asks that we may know God better and more deeply. What if we prayed that way? What might change about our lives if we did?

_____

_____

_____

_____

5. How does the thought that Jesus is above every power on earth make you approach the routine days of life? How does it affect your confidence?

_____

_____

_____

_____

_____

6. Paul knows there are evil forces at work but quickly places them beneath Jesus. How do many Christians envision Christ and evil powers today? How about you?

_____

_____

_____

_____

_____

Invitation and Response

God's Word always invites a response. Think about the way these themes of God's chosen family and the riches of Christ speak to us today. How do they invite us to respond?

God's Word invites us to embrace God's plan for his chosen family, which includes both Jews and gentiles. We can choose to celebrate and be grateful for the inheritance he offers all of us through Christ.

_____

_____

What is your evaluation of yourself based on any or all of the verses found in Ephesians 1?

_____

_____

_____

_____

_____

Paul understood that the future viability
of the church rested on whether it
would be a unified body of believers.

EPHESIANS 2

Ephesians 2 is the chapter where Paul begins to focus on the gentiles whom he is addressing. If chapter 1 is a distant look at the Jewish wing of the church, chapter 2 is a personal look at the gentiles. While Paul is not shy about sharing the ways the gentiles have fallen short, he is purposeful in placing the Jews in the same category as these gentiles. This is a gentle reminder that no ethnicity has favored status in God's family.

A larger purpose in this passage is bringing together the Jews and gentiles into one unified body. Paul uses powerful imagery that describes how Jews and gentiles can be unified and places the risen Christ in the center of this new church. Without unity this new church will fail.

WEEK 2, DAY 1

Absorb the passage in Ephesians 2 by reading it aloud several times until you become familiar with its verses, words, and phrases.

WEEK 2, DAY 2
EPHESIANS 2

The Setting

It has been mentioned previously that Paul was under house arrest as he wrote Ephesians. It was an imprisonment that was initiated by his arrest in Jerusalem because of a disturbance in the temple. Early in his life Paul was widely seen as a zealous and committed Jew. Now near the end of his life Paul was imprisoned because he was viewed as lacking in his commitment to Judaism. Like the leaders of the church in Jerusalem, Paul was a Christian. For most of those leaders Christianity was still part of a larger Jewish faith. Commitment to that ancient faith was still a priority. Paul was arrested in Jerusalem because he was still mistrusted all these years later. The events of that day remained fresh in Paul's memory.

A modern reader can see that Paul was thinking about the temple, and there are many reasons for this claim. First, as a Jew the imagery of the temple would be hard to forget. The ceremonies and design of the temple pointed toward the God of Israel—a God whom Paul believed had taken on flesh. Paul also used the temple as an illustration for his thoughts in Ephesians 2, which is often under-appreciated by commentators on Ephesians.

The Message

As Paul languished in Rome, he realized the dire need for unity in the faith. The lack of unity was one of the reasons Paul was in this situation, and if this church was going to thrive, unity between Jew and gentile would be a necessity. If the larger world would ever be attracted to this faith, unity between groups would be a necessary and attractive feature. This unity moves to the center of Paul's thinking in chapter 2.

Paul not only emphasizes this unity, but he also describes how Jesus Christ brought that unity through his death and resurrection. With his personal trials so prevalent in his life, we should not be surprised that Paul, the Jew, framed his comments with imagery from the temple in Jerusalem. While we can understand Paul's concern in Ephesians, understanding Paul's history and background really brings this letter to life.

To discover the message of Ephesians 2, let's divide the chapter into six sections. Below, summarize or paraphrase the general message or theme of each grouping of verses (following the pattern provided for verses 1–3).

1. Ephesians 2:1–3
Jew and gentile have a common history of sin.

2. Ephesians 2:4–7

3. Ephesians 2:8–10

4. Ephesians 2:11–15a

5. Ephesians 2:15b–18

34

6. Ephesians 2:19–22

WEEK 2, DAY 3

What's Happening in the Passage?

As we read through these passages there are certain ideas and words that were familiar to the original readers but are not as familiar to us. Two thousand years and a vastly different culture obscure some of these ideas from us today. You may encounter some of these words and ideas in your study today. Some of them have been explained in more detail in the **Word Study Notes**. If you want even more detail you can supplement this study with a Bible dictionary or commentary.

1. Ephesians 2:1–3

This is a fairly complex section of Paul's letter, and once again it is important that we remember whom Paul is referencing. In these early sections of chapter 2 Paul continues his comments about the "you" and "us" groups. Paul starts with comments about the "you" group, the gentiles. In his opening sentence Paul made expected comments about the gentiles from a Jewish perspective. Paul states the gentiles were dead in their sins[1]—a position that most Jews would have acknowledged and celebrated.

Before his fellow Jewish believers could feel superior, Paul then begins his unifying words. Paul reminds his readers that the Jews also followed their sinful desires, and were like everyone else, including the gentiles. When Paul placed the Jews on the same level as the gentiles, it would have been an unpopular statement to the Jews, and one that was welcomed by the gentiles. The effect of this statement would be to place both Jew and gentile on the same level before God.

WORD STUDY NOTES #1

[1] We might read the words "trespasses" and "sins" and think that Paul is using two words to describe the same thing for effect, but that is not the case. These two words, *paraptoma* and *hamartia* in Greek, actually describe two different types of wrongdoing, and the difference is important. *Hamartia* is a word that is commonly translated as "sins" but that fails to capture the meaning. *Hamartia* means "missing the intended mark." Shooting an arrow at a bullseye and missing the target is *hamartia*. *Paraptoma* describes a more intentional type of wrongdoing. In Paul's writing, *paraptoma* is a word that is typically used when there is knowledge of the law. Therefore, when Paul uses these two words together, he is describing a full understanding of our wrongdoing. Both Jew and gentile have a history of falling short and purposefully going against God. Both are in view here.

WORD STUDY NOTES #2

[1] In these next verses Paul purposefully starts to bring Jews and gentiles together in Jesus Christ. Paul affirms that Christ has made both groups alive. In case the gentiles miss this point, Paul reminds them that they have been saved through grace. He explains that Jew and gentile have been raised and seated with Christ in the heavenly realms. This is exalted language, but it is meant to unite. Because of what Christ has done, Jews and gentiles can now live in unity, and heaven and earth are united as well. The purpose for the work of Christ was that the life of heaven could start to spread through the united church—a natural result for people who are seated in the heavenly realms. When different ethnic groups and people with differences live together in unity, we hasten every aspect of God's reconciling work.

WORD STUDY NOTES #3

[1] There is a subtle difference in verses 9 and 10 that many fail to notice. In verse 9 Paul uses "works" alone. This is shorthand for the works of the law—a phrase he uses more fully in Galatians 2—which were those things that identified Jews as distinct from the people around them (such as their laws about circumcision, food, Sabbath practices, and more). However, the Jews did not follow the law simply so they could be different. They understood their law as a gift from God, given to protect them, save them, and to honor their covenant with God. Therefore, their obedience in following the law was an act of covenant faithfulness toward God. It was how they showed themselves to be the chosen covenant people of God. They did not follow the law in order to be saved; rather, they had been saved, and as a result, they followed the law. In verse

Create your own brief summary or description of the reality portrayed in verses 4–7.

2. Ephesians 2:4–7[1]

_____

_____

_____

_____

_____

_____

_____

_____

_____

_____

_____

_____

_____

_____

_____

_____

3. Ephesians 2:8–10

In this section Paul reminds the gentiles (you) that their newfound relationship with God is not the result of their own doing. They have been saved through grace, which is the undeserved favor of Christ. Paul also teaches that our status with God is not the result of works.[1] Whether we read this from the ancient Jewish perspective of following the law (or Torah) in order to be a good follower of God, or whether we see it from our contemporary perspective today—that doing good deeds in the world might earn us favor with God—Paul is denouncing all of it. Paul affirms in verse 10 that God's people are to strive for good works—but not to qualify for a certain status with God. We are to do good works in order to be a faithful expression of God's people in the world.

4. Ephesians 2:11–15a

Paul clearly identifies the "you" group here as gentiles. He also identifies their hope as the God of Israel and their inclusion into the family that God started with Abraham. He creates a bleak picture for the gentiles. They are aliens, strangers, and completely without hope. The good news is that, through Christ, the gentiles can now participate in God's family with the Jews.

The problem has always been some people's misunderstanding of the law's purpose. The regulations that marked God's people as special also turned into something that kept them isolated from the gentiles. They could not fulfill their responsibility of being a light to the nations as long as their misunderstanding or misapplication of the law kept them isolated. Paul joyfully proclaims that Christ removed the hostility that exists between Jew and gentile, so the two can now become one.[1]

Summarize what Paul is saying in verses 15b–18.

5. Ephesians 2:15b–18[1, 2]

_____

_____

_____

_____

_____

_____

_____

_____

_____

_____

_____

_____

_____

_____

10 Paul adds a qualifier to the word "works," changing the meaning to "good works." Those who rely on "works of the law" are trusting in their ethnicity to make them saved people of God, instead of trusting in the God who saves. Paul wants the Ephesians to understand that all believers, whether Jew or gentile, are expected to do good deeds in the world around them and that these are not what will save them—only the grace of God will do that.

WORD STUDY NOTES #4

[1] Paul uses imagery from the temple to make his point here. In Herod's Temple in Jerusalem, all people were welcome in the temple courts. It was a large and impressive structure that could hold tens of thousands of people. Within the larger temple structure there was an inner court where only the Jews were allowed. This inner area was marked by a low, three-foot-high wall that separated the Jewish court from the larger, more inclusive area. When Paul uses the term "dividing wall," he has this dividing partition in mind. No ethnic group has favored access to God in the church of Jesus Christ. All are equal.

WORD STUDY NOTES #5

[1] In case his readers fail to understand the point he has been making, Paul makes the point even more forcefully. The wall of partition has been destroyed by Christ. A reinterpretation of what it means to follow the law is now required so that Jew and gentile might become the one, unified body of Christ.

[2] There are times when we hear the call for political unity, or a plea for people to be in agreement. Paul's words go beyond this call. He has a far greater vision for God's people. Our unity is to be built around a person. We are unified when Jew and gentile both proclaim

Christ and order our lives around the crucified Christ. It is not a call for mental unity or simple agreement but a spiritual call for sacrificial living.

[1] Paul may have an even larger purpose here. One of the saddest visions in the Old Testament is presented in Ezekiel, when the glory of the Lord leaving the temple is described. The purpose of the book of Ezekiel, then, is to prepare the people of God for the return of the glory of God. With this language in Ephesians 2, Paul is describing the very same thing. When God's people are united, God's presence inhabits his newly reconstructed temple, which is not a physical building but a spiritual temple on earth made possible by Christ and consisting of Jew and gentile together.

6. Ephesians 2:19–22

Following complex language distinguishing Jew and gentile, Paul's unifying vision is finally complete, and now Paul can use exalted language to describe the new reality. Too often the modern reader misses Paul's great vision here. Strangers and aliens (gentiles) and saints (Jews) are citizens together. Apostles (post-Christ) and prophets (pre-Christ) both serve as the foundation, but Christ is the unifying force for it all.

Paul has spent the early part of chapter 2 tearing down the dividing wall in Herod's Temple,[1] and abolishing the regulations that divide Jews from the rest of the world. Yet Paul does not have destructive aims in mind. His larger theme is that God has created a new temple, and the church bears witness to this new creation.

Discoveries

Let's summarize our discoveries from Ephesians 2.

1. Paul reminded the Jews they were dead in their sins just as the gentiles were.

2. Paul also reminded the gentiles that they are part of God's family just as the Jews are.

3. We are reminded that while we are not saved as a result of our own doing, we are created to do good works as representatives of Christ.

4. Believers are reminded that a concern for our own holiness can lead us to separate ourselves from those we are supposed to reach.

5. We have seen that the unified church is the new temple in which the presence of God dwells.

Unity in the Church and the Story of God

Whenever we read a biblical text, it is important to ask how the particular text we are reading relates to the rest of the Bible. Ephesians is written toward the end of Paul's life and ministry. Paul's public life as a leader was about fully including the gentiles in the life of the church. This early struggle was a theme in many other parts of the New Testament. We can trace this important struggle by looking at other passages in the New Testament where the unity of the church is highlighted.

Places in Scripture where this theme is notably present include but are not limited to Acts 15:1–10, 22–29, Galatians 2:15–21, Colossians 2:6–23, 1 Peter 2:4–12, and Revelation 21:1–14. **In the space given below, write a short summary of how the theme of unity in the church shows up in each passage.**

Acts 15:1–10

_____

_____

_____

_____

_____

Acts 15:22–29

_____

_____

_____

_____

_____

_____

If you have a study Bible, it may have references in a margin, a middle column, or footnotes that point to other biblical texts. You may find it helpful in understanding how the whole story of God ties together to look up some of those other scriptures from time to time.

40

Galatians 2:15–21

_____

_____

_____

_____

_____

_____

Colossians 2:6–23

_____

_____

_____

_____

_____

_____

1 Peter 2:4–12

_____

_____

_____

_____

_____

_____

Revelation 21:1–14

_____

_____

_____

_____

_____

_____

WEEK 2, DAY 5

Ephesians and Our World Today

When we look at the theme of unity in the church in Ephesians 2, it can become the lens through which we see ourselves, our world, and how God works in our world today.

1. While we no longer fight the Jew/gentile question, are there other groups we exclude from the church?

Sometimes we exclude people who are different from us for various reasons—even other Christians.

God desired unity for the Jews and gentiles during Paul's lifetime, and God also desires unity

for us now.

_____

_____

Following the above example, answer these questions about how we can understand ourselves, our world, and God's action in our world today.

2. What would have to change for us to fully include these excluded groups from the church?

_____

_____

_____

_____

_____

_____

3. What walls keep us from reaching out to the ones who might need Christ?

_____

_____

_____

_____

_____

_____

4. Do we still fight the outdated faith-versus-works battle? How might this inhibit some from pursuing good works?

_____

_____

_____

_____

_____

5. We typically speak the language of the Spirit dwelling in individual believers. How does the imagery of the Spirit dwelling in the corporate body of believers impact our view of God?

_____

_____

_____

_____

_____

Invitation and Response

God's Word always invites a response. Think about the way the theme of unity in the church speaks to us today. How does it invite us to respond?

Paul's message in Ephesians 2 invites us to not only receive the peace we are given through Christ's rescue of our souls but also to live out that peace in our relationships with others. We can look for opportunities to be united with those who are different from us through the faith we share.

_____

What is your evaluation of yourself based on any or all of the verses found in Ephesians 2?

_____

_____

_____

_____

_____

Without unity the church will fail.

EPHESIANS 3

This is one of the most inspiring chapters in the New Testament. Paul has just spent the previous two chapters describing the importance of Jews and gentiles being unified in the church and explaining how that unification is possible through Jesus Christ. With this unified church so prominent in his mind, Paul prays a significant prayer for these new Jewish and gentile believers. We should pay attention to the things that Paul prays for—it may sound different from many of our prayers today.

WEEK 3, DAY 1

Absorb the passage in Ephesians 3 by reading it aloud several times until you become familiar with its verses, words, and phrases.

WEEK 3, DAY 2

EPHESIANS 3

The Setting

In chapter 2 the setting was the temple in Jerusalem. The vision of the physical temple served as a background for Paul's thinking. In chapter 3 the background moves to a much larger vision. Paul moves from the first-century temple in Jerusalem to a picture of the entire world. The division between Jew and gentile has been rectified in chapter 2, and the new conflict is the unified church and its battle with both the political forces of the day and the spiritual forces that stand behind their political allies.

The pastoral side of Paul also emerges in chapter 3. Even though he does not personally know these churches, Paul deeply cares for these believers. This love is seen in the qualities that Paul desires these believers acquire. The chapter closes with the imprisoned Paul launching into a great pastoral prayer for these believers.

The Message

In the first two chapters of Ephesians Paul establishes the reasons why the gentiles and Jews are unified in Christ. Having demonstrated the reason for this unity, Paul moves to explaining why unity is so vital in the church. It is undoubtedly true that Paul would have considered unity an important trait for the health of any local church, but there were much larger reasons why Paul thinks it is important.

There was a battle that was being waged, and it was larger than any local church. It was also a battle that involved the church and the Roman emperor and a battle that featured the unseen spiritual forces that stand against the church. When different ethnic groups live in unity, that unity is a weapon that diminishes the forces that stand against the church. This issue is so vital that it moves Paul to pray one of the great prayers of the New Testament. It is a prayer for unity, and a prayer that all of God's people will experience all the gifts God gives.

To discover the message of Ephesians 3, let's divide the chapter into four sections
**Below, summarize or paraphrase the general message or theme of each grouping of
verses (following the pattern provided for verses 1–4).**

1. Ephesians 3:1–4
Paul is in chains. Even while in prison Paul is being used by God.

_____

_____

2. Ephesians 3:5–7

_____

_____

_____

_____

_____

_____

3. Ephesians 3:8–13

_____

_____

_____

_____

_____

_____

4. Ephesians 3:14–21

_____

_____

_____

_____

_____

_____

_____

WEEK 3, DAY 3

What's Happening in the Passage?

As we read through these passages there are certain ideas and words that were familiar to the original readers but are not as familiar to us. Two thousand years and a vastly different culture obscure some of these ideas from us today. You may encounter some of these words and ideas in your study today. Some of them have been explained in more detail in the **Word Study Notes**. If you want even more detail you can supplement this study with a Bible dictionary or commentary.

1. Ephesians 3:1–4[1]

While undoubtedly these churches knew of Paul's reputation, this was his chance to introduce himself to these new believers. Even if he had not visited these churches, Paul wants them to know that his current imprisonment is linked to his work on behalf of the gentiles, and that he cares enough about their inclusion that he is willing to be in chains for this cause. He also wants them to know that God was the one who sent him to the gentiles. The grace of Jesus Christ was given to Paul so he could complete this important task.

Create your own brief summary or description of the reality portrayed in verses 5–7.

2. Ephesians 3:5–7[1]

_____

_____

_____

_____

_____

_____

_____

_____

WORD STUDY NOTES #1

[1] The irony is so apparent in these words. Paul was not just any person. He was an exemplary Jew in every way. He had been zealous for his beloved Judaism and spent a portion of his life protecting it from all sorts of troublesome ideas from the gentiles. Yet God has selected Paul to include the gentiles in his new church. If a zealous leader of the Jews can accept the gentiles, it is possible for anyone.

WORD STUDY NOTES #2

[1] In Ephesians 3 Paul keeps referencing a mystery, and it is a word we might not expect to find in the New Testament. It is a word that Paul probably borrowed from Asia Minor. There were religions there, like the Artemis cult in Ephesus, that focused on the mysteries of the divine and held in high esteem those who claimed to know the mysteries. People pursued these "mysteries," so Paul imports this word and uses it for his own purposes. Since Paul was specifically commissioned by God to take the gospel to the gentiles, he can proclaim what he calls a mystery—that the gentiles are fully included in God's family, and they are members of the same body. They do not have to sit at a different table but are fully integrated. This "mystery" is now apparent to anyone who wishes to see.

WORD STUDY NOTES #3

[1] One of the issues that a modern reader faces is what to do with the phrase "rulers and authorities in the heavenly realms." We immediately think of demonic and evil forces that are informed by Hollywood and modern stories, but this was not the world of Paul. In the Palestinian Judaism of this

time the enemies of Israel were well known. In ancient Jewish literature the ethnic and national enemies of Israel were supported by Belial and other evil forces in the spiritual realm. Israel had to do battle on both a political and cosmic scale.

[2] Believers can approach Christ with confidence because we have been seated with him in the heavens, and when we live in unity, we have a certain victory over the forces that stand opposed to us. When we participate in factions, we are still subject to earthly rulers. When gentiles are fully included and welcomed into the church, the gospel is announced to the rulers and authorities, and the spiritual forces that once waged war with God's people are shaken and unnerved. The battle that was proclaimed finished on the cross is finished in the spiritual realms as well, so Paul wants his readers to live according to their heavenly status granted through Christ and not their earthly concerns.

WORD STUDY NOTES #4

[1] The theme of unity permeates this great prayer Paul prays for these believers. The Father is God of every family and all God's holy people.

[2] Paul uses a term that would have been familiar to these believers in Asia Minor. Paul prays that they might be filled to the level of the fullness of God. The word "fullness" *(pleroma)* was a religious term used

3. Ephesians 3:8–13

The corporate church is the focus in this passage. The unity of Jew and gentile is more than just a nice goal; it is a trait of cosmic importance. Paul is aware of the forces that stand against the church as well as the weapons at its disposal. When we live in unity, we announce to all political rulers and spiritual forces that stand behind them[1] that Jesus Christ is Lord. Without the inclusion of the gentiles, the church cannot make such a grand statement.[2]

Summarize what Paul is saying in verses 14–21.

4. Ephesians 3:14–21[1, 2]

_____

_____

_____

_____

_____

_____

_____

_____

_____

_____

_____

_____

_____

_____

_____

_____

_____

Discoveries

Let's summarize our discoveries from Ephesians 3.

1. Paul was a zealous Jew who spent his ministry reaching out to gentiles.

2. The mystery that Paul mentions is the full inclusion of gentiles into the family of God.

3. Paul realizes the extent and strength of the enemy that stands opposed to the church.

4. Paul wants believers to know that Christ is the embodiment of all the divine qualities.

5. From this point forward Paul wants believers to know that Jews and gentiles are full participants in the church.

6. The primary quality of God's people should always be love.

in the Gnostic world to represent the entity between the godhead and creation that contained all the divine deities or attributes. In the Gnostic godhead, one of the spirit deities was Christ. It was believed that one acquired fullness through a certain level of knowledge of the divine within each person. Paul takes this concept and applies it to God. One does not gain fullness by knowing oneself better; one gains this fullness by experiencing the great love of God.

If you have a study Bible, it may have references in a margin, a middle column, or footnotes that point to other biblical texts. You may find it helpful in understanding how the whole story of God ties together to look up some of those other scriptures from time to time.

The Indwelling of the Spirit and the Story of God

Whenever we read a biblical text, it is important to ask how the particular text we are reading relates to the rest of the Bible. In chapter 3 Paul prays that these believers may know the reality of the Holy Spirit living in them. This is not just an isolated prayer in Ephesians 3 but a consistent feature within the Bible. We can discover places both in the Old Testament and New Testament where this indwelling presence of the Holy Spirit is emphasized.

Places in Scripture where this theme is notably present include but are not limited to Joel 2:28–32, Jeremiah 31:31–34, John 14:15–27, Acts 2:1–13, Romans 8:1–17, and 2 Corinthians 1:22–23. **In the space given below, summarize how each passage utilizes the theme of the Spirit's indwelling.**

Joel 2:28–32

_____

_____

_____

_____

_____

_____

Jeremiah 31:31–34

_____

_____

_____

_____

_____

_____

_____

John 14:15–27

_____

_____

_____

_____

_____

_____

_____

Acts 2:1–13

_____

_____

_____

_____

_____

Romans 8:1–17

_____

_____

_____

_____

_____

2 Corinthians 1:21–23

_____

_____

_____

_____

_____

WEEK 3, DAY 5

Ephesians and Our World Today

When we look at the theme of the indwelling of the Spirit in Ephesians 3, it can become the lens through which we see ourselves, our world, and how God works in our world today.

1. If you were a gentile and received a letter from the ex-Jewish persecutor of the new Christian church, how would you receive it?

It might take a while to trust someone who had done so much harm in their past. We don't

I always appreciate the struggle Paul had; he would not have been received warmly in many

places due to his reputation.

Following the above example, answer these questions about how we can understand ourselves, our world, and God's action in our world today.

2. Why would a Jew like Paul refer to the inclusion of the gentiles as a mystery?

3. How does the thought that believers are elevated with Christ into the heavens impact your faith?

4. In what ways does the unity of believers make a statement to the greater world?

_____

_____

_____

_____

_____

5. What is a danger of looking within ourselves to find the divine?

_____

_____

_____

_____

6. Why is love so elevated in the writing of Paul as compared to almost every other trait?

_____

_____

_____

_____

_____

Invitation and Response

God's Word always invites a response. Think about the way the theme of the Spirit's indwelling speaks to us today. How does it invite us to respond?

God's Word calls us to dive deep into the mystery of the gospel and experience the vast love of God made known to us through Jesus Christ. Through Paul's prayer for the Ephesians, we are invited to slow down and take the time needed to get to know the Holy Spirit who fills us so we can live out the gospel.

_____

_____

_____

What is your evaluation of yourself based on any or all of the verses found in
Ephesians 2?

_____

_____

_____

_____

_____

_____

_____

_____

_____

_____

_____

_____

_____

_____

_____

_____

_____

_____

_____

_____

_____

_____

_____

The primary quality of
God's people should
always be love.

EPHESIANS 4:1-24

In his profound prayer from chapter 3, Paul has just prayed that his readers may be filled to the measure of all the fullness of God. The question that follows is *what should the believers do now that they have been filled?* Here in chapter 4 Paul answers that we should live out of this fullness corporately in an effort to maintain unity. We are not divided along the Jew/gentile lines of Ephesians, but we still allow other fault lines to divide us in the church. Paul reminds his readers to not let this happen.

Paul also looks back to the former way of life of these gentiles. To the modern ear this may sound like Paul is being unduly harsh, but it was the gentiles who were recently living in pagan ways, unlike the Jews. This is a simple reminder that we should not let former habits or patterns back into our lives. We should live differently, and our lives should be characterized by our new reality, which is found in Christ.

WEEK 4, DAY 1

Absorb the passage in Ephesians 4:1–24 by reading it aloud several times until you become familiar with its verses, words, and phrases.

WEEK 4, DAY 2

EPHESIANS 4:1-24

The Setting

At this point in Ephesians a shift occurs, and Paul begins the part of the letter that contains practical advice. Paul has just finished a great prayer for these believers, imploring that they might know the great love that God has for them and be unified. With this call for unity fresh in the readers' minds, Paul begins chapter 4.

The Message

While this passage would seem to be the beginning of his practical instructions, it actually serves as almost a transition. Before he can start these instructions in earnest, Paul reaffirms the unity of the faith and the oneness of God. He then moves to a creative application of Psalm 68 that leaves some readers puzzled. Paul makes frequent use of Old Testament scriptures in his teachings, and he often reinterprets them, following the example of Jesus in departing from tradition to offer a new application of Scripture, and that is what he is doing here with Psalm 68.

To discover the message of Ephesians 4:1–24, let's divide the passage into six sections. **Below, summarize or paraphrase the general message or theme of each grouping of verses (following the pattern provided for verses 7–10).**

1. Ephesians 4:1–6

_____

_____

_____

_____

_____

_____

2. Ephesians 4:7–10

Paul is introducing the next set of verses here by placing all authority with Christ

(who has authority even over death) to give us grace and spiritual gifts.

_____

3. Ephesians 4:11–13

_____

_____

_____

_____

_____

_____

4. Ephesians 4:14–16

_____

_____

_____

_____

_____

_____

5. Ephesians 4:17–19

_____

_____

_____

_____

_____

_____

_____

_____

6. Ephesians 4:20–24

_____

_____

_____

_____

_____

[1]In this passage Paul is quoting from Psalm 68, but he has reinterpreted the psalm. In Psalm 68, a passage about the Lord ascending to Zion, gifts are received by the Lord and not given. It is a picture of the Lord leading the captives—Israel's enemies—and receiving tribute from them. This leads to the obvious question of why Paul uses this psalm in the way he does. It seems probable that he does it to make a point, which was common in rabbinical interpretations. Since the Spirit has already been introduced and used freely in Ephesians, the work of Christ and the Spirit seems to be a good background for this passage. Christ ascended to the heavens; as a result the Spirit was able to descend, and the presence of the Spirit brings gifts to God's people.

[2] Much confusion has resulted from reading this passage through the lens of the later Apostles' Creed. In this rendering of the passage the "descended" of verses 9–10 refers to Jesus's journey to hell between his death and Easter morning. This is to be doubted for two reasons. First, this would be an improper interpretation of *hades*, which in the Old Testament simply referred to "the grave." Paul is certain that Christ has conquered death. Secondly, Paul has already made clear that these

WEEK 4, DAY 3

What's Happening in the Passage?

As we read through these passages there are certain ideas and words that were familiar to the original readers but are not as familiar to us. Two thousand years and a vastly different culture obscure some of these ideas from us today. You may encounter some of these words and ideas in your study today. Some of them have been explained in more detail in the **Word Study Notes**. If you want even more detail you can supplement this study with a Bible dictionary or commentary.

1. Ephesians 4:1–6

Paul returns to his beloved Scriptures to advance his argument. One can hear the echo of Deuteronomy 6:4 in his words: "Hear O Israel: the LORD our God, the LORD is one." If there is one Lord, then our faith should be unified as well. Paul makes another point: If the gentiles and Jews remain divided, how can we make the claim that Jesus is Lord of the whole earth? If Jew and gentile are not unified, then God is only a god for the Jews, which is a point Paul makes explicitly in Romans 2.

Paul also recalls the other parts of our faith that bear witness to unity. Regardless of our ethnicity or place of origin, all of us submit to one faith and one baptism. Paul's simple plea is that the rest of our Christian life bears witness to the unity our faith exemplifies.

Create your own brief summary or description of the reality portrayed in verses 7–10.

2. Ephesians 4:7–10[1, 2]

_____

_____

_____

_____

3. Ephesians 4:11–13

Not all of us have the same talents and abilities, nor should we expect to. Whatever our ability, we are called to use our gifts for the good of the church. In a world that is filled with people seeking selfish gain, God's people should be marked by our desire to build each other up.

Summarize what Paul is saying in verses 14–16.

4. Ephesians 4:14–16[1]

_____

_____

_____

_____

_____

_____

_____

_____

_____

_____

_____

_____

_____

_____

5. Ephesians 4:17–19

At first this passage might seem insensitive, but there is an important message here. Remember, Paul is writing the words "no longer live as the Gentiles¹ do" to gentiles. Paul is not denigrating gentiles as a group of people but is reminding these believers that their lives should change when they follow Christ. It is a problem when our lives still look the same after following Christ.

powers and authorities Christ defeated exist in the "heavenly realms," not a place beneath the earthly regions. The ascent and descent in this passage should be seen as a description of the incarnation, where Christ did descend to live among his people.

WORD STUDY NOTES #4

[1] The word "mature" here is the same one used in Matthew 5:48 and translated "perfect." This word, _teleos_, simply means "whole and complete, reaching full maturity." If we do not use our gifts for the benefit of the whole church, we fail to reach maturity as a people.

WORD STUDY NOTES #5

[1] Paul's reference to gentiles here may not refer to the ethnicity of gentiles but a spiritual quality. The term "hardening of their hearts" is a common biblical metaphor, most famously used in reference to Pharaoh in the Exodus story. This term usually describes extreme insensitivity that comes from a repetition of wrong choices. It does not happen by accident but is a purposeful rejection of God's call.

Word Study Notes #6

[1]This passage refers back to Ephesians 2:15 and Paul's words that God has made a new humanity. Because of the death and resurrection of Christ, believers have a new identity. Our identity in Christ supersedes every ethnic and national identity that defines us in other ways. When we fail to live according to our new identity, we return back to the old self, or old life.

6. Ephesians 4:20-24

Paul reminds his readers that we participate in the new life that Christ brings.[1] Yes, God changes us, but we play an active part in that change. We have to "put off" some old habits, which implies intentional action on our part. We are also commanded to "put on" the new. God will never change us over our own objections. We must play an active role in this new life.

Discoveries

Let's summarize our discoveries from Ephesians 4:1–24.

1. The powers that Christ triumphs over are also in the heavenly realms.

2. When Paul quotes from the Old Testament about the day Jesus descended, a journey to hell is not being described.

3. The church reaches maturity when all of us use our gifts in the service of Christ.

4. When Paul instructs his readers to no longer live like the gentiles, he is referencing those who live without Christ, not the entire ethnic group.

5. Believers are not passive participants in the Christian life; we play an active role in our own growth.

Maturity in Christ and the Story of God

Whenever we read a biblical text, it is important to ask how the particular text we are reading relates to the rest of the Bible. The idea of maturity as a goal of the Christian life is not new in Scripture. This might be a good time to explore instances in the New Testament where maturity or wholeness is described.

Places in Scripture where this theme is notably present include but are not limited to Matthew 5:43–48, 19:21, Romans 12:1–3, 1 Corinthians 13:9–11, Colossians 1:28, James 1:4, and 1 John 4:12. **In the space given below, summarize how each passage utilizes the theme of maturity in Christ.**

Matthew 5:43–48

_____

_____

_____

_____

_____

Matthew 19:21

_____

_____

_____

_____

_____

Romans 12:1–3

_____

_____

_____

_____

_____

If you have a study Bible, it may have references in a margin, a middle column, or footnotes that point to other biblical texts. You may find it helpful in understanding how the whole story of God ties together to look up some of those other scriptures from time to time.

1 Corinthians 13:9–11

_____

_____

_____

_____

_____

_____

Colossians 1:28

_____

_____

_____

_____

_____

_____

James 1:4

_____

_____

_____

_____

_____

_____

1 John 4:12

_____

_____

_____

_____

_____

_____

WEEK 4, DAY 5

Ephesians and Our World Today

When we look at the theme of maturity in Christ in Ephesians 4:1–24, it can become the lens through which we see ourselves, our world, and how God works in our world today.

1. When reminded to live a life that is worthy, are we living to qualify for God's grace or in response to God's grace?

We always live in grateful response. The life that is always trying to qualify is a joyless Christian life. We are called to live in relationship and in gratitude for what has already been done for us.

_____

Following the above example, answer these questions about how we can understand ourselves, our world, and God's action in our world today.

2. Why is unity so important to Paul?

_____
_____
_____
_____

3. When Paul says, "you must no longer live like the gentiles do," what does he mean?

_____
_____
_____
_____

4. Paul compares a lack of unity with being like "infants." In what ways is this true?

_____
_____
_____
_____

5. What are some dangers in thinking that we play no part in developing Christian character?

_____

_____

_____

_____

_____

_____

_____

Invitation and Response

God's Word always invites a response. Think about the way the theme of maturity in Christ speaks to us today. How does it invite us to respond?

Paul is inviting us to consider that we have a choice in becoming mature and whole in Christ.

We get to be actively involved in our own spiritual growth. When we engage our will to "put on the

new self," we are sharing the gift of our life in Christ with the world.

_____

_____

What is your evaluation of yourself based on any or all of the verses found in Ephesians 4:1–24?

_____

_____

_____

_____

_____

_____

_____

_____

_____

Believers are not passive participants
in the Christian life; we play an
active role in our own growth.

EPHESIANS 4:25–5:20

This passage starts with the often-used "therefore" by Paul, linking these verses to what immediately comes before. In the preceding section Paul has commanded his readers to no longer live like the gentiles who are without Christ. He also told his readers to "put on the new self" that is possible because of Christ. Perhaps anticipating a question of what that means, Paul provides specific answers starting in verse 25.

WEEK 5, DAY 1

Absorb the passage in Ephesians 4:25–5:20 by reading it aloud several times until you become familiar with its verses, words, and phrases.

WEEK 5, DAY 2

EPHESIANS 4:25-5:20

The Setting

Paul has called believers into a new kind of life that matches their position of being seated with Christ. Paul desires that these gentiles should live differently from the people around them. They must make decisions on what not to do anymore, as well as what to do. This is the point in the letter when Paul moves from a general appeal to a more specific list of expectations for these new Christians. But, lest we fall into the same trap that the Jews were at risk of falling into if they misunderstood the law (as we discussed in Week Two), let's make it clear up front that Paul is not saying new Christians must behave in certain ways in order to be accepted by God. Rather, Paul is saying that they have been accepted by God already, and their new status with Christ should make them want to change the way they live.

The Message

There are some who might question Paul's methods in these verses. Paul, the opponent of legalistic living in Galatians, seems to establish a fairly specific list of dos and don'ts in this passage. We need to remember that Paul was familiar with the church in Galatia—a church that had intensive, firsthand knowledge of Paul. The churches to whom Ephesians was addressed had no such knowledge of Paul. We should also remember that these are brand-new churches fresh from their pagan history. Paul specifically names behaviors that will prove deeply problematic to any emerging church.

To discover the message of Ephesians 4:25–5:20, let's divide the passage into six sections. **Below, summarize or paraphrase the general message or theme of each grouping of verses (following the pattern provided for 5:3–7).**

1. Ephesians 4:25–28

_____

_____

_____

_____

_____

_____

_____

2. Ephesians 4:29–32

_____

_____

_____

_____

_____

3. Ephesians 5:1–2

_____

_____

_____

_____

_____

4. Ephesians 5:3–7

The Roman world of the first century shares many traits with our world today. Our modern moral environment is nothing new.

_____

_____

_____

5. Ephesians 5:8–14

_____

_____

_____

_____

_____

6. Ephesians 5:15–20

_____

_____

_____

_____

WEEK 5, DAY 3

What's Happening in the Passage?

As we read through these passages there are certain ideas and words that were familiar to the original readers but are not as familiar to us. Two thousand years and a vastly different culture obscure some of these ideas from us today. You may encounter some of these words and ideas in your study today. Some of them have been explained in more detail in the **Word Study Notes**. If you want even more detail you can supplement this study with a Bible dictionary or commentary.

Create your own brief description of Paul's words in 4:25–28.

1. Ephesians 4:25–28[1]

_____
_____
_____
_____
_____
_____
_____

2. Ephesians 4:29–32

Paul gets very specific about other behaviors to avoid. The primary warning is for believers to be careful with their words. Our words have the power to both heal and harm. Our comments can welcome and wound, so we must be careful. When Paul tells his readers to "get rid of" these negative traits in verse 31, he is using passive voice in the Greek, which indicates that believers need the power of the Spirit[1] in their struggle against their own weaknesses.

WORD STUDY NOTES #1

[1] There is a tendency to believe that Christians should never get angry, but that is not the perspective of Paul in chapter 4. This is a passage that takes anger seriously and recognizes that anger is a reality. In fact, God's people *should* see things that anger them in the fallen world in which they live. At the same time Paul recognizes that anger poses a danger for the Christian, so he sets a time limit for anger to linger. What provokes anger should be addressed promptly and never allowed to fester. Paul warns of more serious consequences if anger is allowed to linger—the devil might be able to exploit anger and use it for his own ends. Paul's advice is to never allow the enemy that foothold.

WORD STUDY NOTES #2

[1] In this passage Paul gives an ominous warning about grieving the Holy Spirit. By doing so Paul emphasizes that the Spirit is not an impersonal force but a personal presence in the life of the church. Throughout the passage Paul has highlighted the work of the Spirit in building up the body of Christ. When we use words to tear down that body, we are doing more than causing trouble; we are personally acting against the God who desires to bless and build up the church.

[1] In contrast with those who are tearing down the body, Paul holds up the crucified Christ as our example. Christ willingly sacrificed for the church and gave himself for her redemption. Since believers are supposed to imitate Christ, we are also called to sacrifice for each other and for the good of the church, for whom Christ died.

3. Ephesians 5:1–2[1]

_____

_____

_____

_____

_____

_____

_____

_____

_____

_____

_____

_____

_____

_____

_____

_____

WORD STUDY NOTES #4

[1] At this point in the letter Paul metaphorically turns up the heat on his readers. If we continue to live in a disobedient and sinful manner, we invite God's wrath. Paul uses the present tense in his description of God's wrath, which could indicate both the present experience of those who are disobedient and their possible future. This might seem harsh, but Paul's intent is to root out sinful behavior in the community of faith. There should be no lowering of any standard within the church. Everything is at stake for the believer.

4. Ephesians 5:3–7

Paul lists another specific problem—a problem of which "there must not be even a hint." Paul broadly condemns sexual immorality, which can refer to any sexual vice. This was written during a time when it was difficult to draw proper boundaries around sexual activities. The Roman Empire was not known for its moral conduct. Paul desires to stress that greed for sexual indulgence is never fitting for God's people. Paul also adds that we should be careful with immoral or foolish talk. The danger is that talk may offend those around us and lead to disobedience.[1] In an effort to guard against a life of empty talk, we should endeavor to fill our talk with words of thanksgiving and gratitude.

Write out a paraphrase of Paul's teaching in 5:8–14.

5. Ephesians 5:8–14[1]

_____

_____

_____

_____

_____

_____

_____

_____

_____

_____

_____

_____

_____

_____

_____

_____

_____

6. Ephesians 5:15–20

This is another passage that contains a familiar concept. After a chapter listing numerous behaviors that cause problems for the church,[1] Paul implores them to be filled with the Spirit instead. The antidote to these behaviors is not a corresponding list of replacement qualities but an internal presence that transforms life from the inside out. As we saw earlier, this call for an encounter with the indwelling Holy Spirit is not new with Paul but was found in the Old Testament prophets as well. This life in the Spirit has become Paul's central focus, replacing his previous pursuit of the law.

WORD STUDY NOTES #5

[1] Echoing other biblical language, Paul calls these believers "children of light." This imagery has a dual meaning. Believers are to be contrasted with those who do not know Christ and still walk in darkness. Since we are children of light, we should live our lives in a transparent manner, as those whose lives are in full view.

WORD STUDY NOTES #6

[1] We live in times of comfort and relative wealth, especially when compared to almost every other time in human history. It is easy to forget that we live in a time that Paul calls evil. This should be understood in contrast with the coming reign and kingdom of God. Even in good times we exist in a world that is fallen, bearing the marks of decay, disease, and death. In every circumstance of life, the enemy can place obstacles in the way of believers. This realization should prompt us to live carefully.

Discoveries

Let's summarize our discoveries from Ephesians 4:25–5:20.

1. Paul does not condemn all forms of anger; instead he warns his readers about letting anger linger.

2. We are reminded about the personal nature of the Holy Spirit, and when we allow division in the church we grieve the Holy Spirit.

3. The original readers of Ephesians lived in a time of moral laxity, so Paul warns his readers to avoid all forms of sexual immorality.

4. Paul encourages his readers to be filled with the Holy Spirit. We do not go into battle alone but with the indwelling presence of God.

WEEK 5, DAY 4

Walking in the Light and the Story of God

Whenever we read a biblical text, it is important to ask how the particular text we are reading relates to the rest of the Bible. There is a strong contrast in this passage between those who follow Christ and those who remain in the world. Those who follow Christ are walking in the light, as opposed to those who remain in darkness. This is a theme that is prevalent in other areas of the New Testament as well.

Places in Scripture where this theme is notably present include but are not limited to Matthew 5:14–16, John 3:19–21, 12:35-36, 2 Corinthians 4:4–6, 1 John 1:5–7, and Revelation 21:23–24. **In the space given below, summarize how each passage utilizes the theme of walking in the light.**

Matthew 5:14–16

_____

_____

_____

_____

_____

_____

John 3:19–21

_____

_____

_____

_____

_____

_____

_____

If you have a study Bible, it may have references in a margin, a middle column, or footnotes that point to other biblical texts. You may find it helpful in understanding how the whole story of God ties together to look up some of those other scriptures from time to time.

John 12:35–36

_____
_____
_____
_____
_____
_____

2 Corinthians 4:4–6

_____
_____
_____
_____
_____
_____

1 John 1:5–7

_____
_____
_____
_____
_____
_____

Revelation 21:23–24

_____
_____
_____
_____
_____
_____

WEEK 5, DAY 5

Ephesians and Our World Today

When we look at the theme of walking in the light in Ephesians 4:25–5:20, it can become the lens through which we see ourselves, our world, and how God works in our world today.

1. Anger is not always a sinful expression. When would Paul consider it to be a problem?

When sin is not dealt with immediately and is allowed to linger, then it is a problem. The problem is that we are creating an entry point for the enemy to pursue the anger instead of Christ. Anger is not wrong; allowing it to take a foothold is.

Following the above example, answer these questions about how we can understand ourselves, our world, and God's action in our world today.

2. In what ways does the Spirit enable us to overcome the enemy?

3. Would Paul think his warning against foolish talk is still necessary today?

4. Why do you think Paul included a warning about God's wrath in this letter?

_____

_____

_____

_____

_____

_____

_____

_____

5. Do you think most Christians think that our days are evil?

_____

_____

_____

_____

_____

_____

_____

_____

6. What are the dangers of holding our times in too high an esteem?

_____

_____

_____

_____

_____

_____

_____

_____

Invitation and Response

God's Word always invites a response. Think about the way the theme of walking in the light speaks to us today. How does it invite us to respond?

Paul instructs us to "walk in the way of love" (Ephesians 5:2) because we know we are loved by God. By walking in the light, we are doing our part to keep the door shut to the enemy's attempts to steal, kill, and destroy.

What is your evaluation of yourself based on any or all of the verses found in Ephesians 4:25–5:20?

When we allow division in the church we grieve the Holy Spirit.

EPHESIANS 5:21-6:9

Paul gave specific instructions to the believers around Ephesus in the preceding passages, and now he focuses his teaching on how to be people of God in homes and within families. In the preceding verses Paul warned against succumbing to sexual immorality—we can be sure that marriages and homes were under attack in Paul's day, just as they are in our own. Paul wants his advice to be remembered and practiced, so he places the advice in a familiar pattern for these gentile believers. Regardless of how every other aspect of life unfolds, it is impossible to live a triumphant life if our homes do not bear the marks of Christ.

85

Absorb the passage in Ephesians 5:21–6:9 by reading it aloud several times until you become familiar with its verses, words, and phrases.

WEEK 6, DAY 2

EPHESIANS 5:21-6:9

The Setting

It is important to remember that this passage of Ephesians was written within the context of larger Greco-Roman society. Like almost all ancient cultures, the Greco-Roman culture was dominated by men—specifically the male head of the household, or *paterfamilias*. He was to rule over the affairs of the household, and each person in the household was to live in relation to the male head.

Many Greek writers wrote on the affairs of their society in something called a "household code." Plato wrote one, as did Aristotle and many other Greek writers. When a modern reader reads this section of Ephesians, it is vital to not make the mistake of reading as if it were written to the twenty-first century. We must read it in light of the ancient world in general, and the genre of the household code in particular.

The Message

In this section of Ephesians Paul continues giving his readers practical advice. Yet the advice gets intensely personal, so Paul uses the long-established form of the household code to deliver it. This is undoubtedly because it would have been a familiar format and made it much more readable to the ancient audience.

In other household codes the format was simple. All instructions for the household were given to the *paterfamilias*, and it was his role to manage every relationship in the house. In Greek household codes, there was no direct address of women, children, or any slaves. In each case these members of the household were seen as unfit to receive direct instruction. The slaves had no standing, the children were under the control of the head of the household, and the women were constitutionally incapable, since they were seen as the weaker sex. When we read this passage written by Paul, we should see where he is similar to the other codes, and where he is surprisingly different. The places where Paul is different are the places where he is distinguishing Christianity from the larger culture, and we should take notice.

To discover the message of Ephesians 5:21–6:9, let's divide the passage into five sections. Below, summarize or paraphrase the general message or theme of each grouping of verses (following the pattern provided for 5:25–28).

1. Ephesians 5:21–24

_____

_____

_____

_____

_____

_____

_____

_____

_____

2. Ephesians 5:25–28

Paul thought the command to love was important in the first century. This command is still

relevant in our time.

_____

_____

_____

3. Ephesians 5:29–33

_____

_____

_____

_____

_____

_____

_____

_____

_____

4. Ephesians 6:1–4

_____
_____
_____
_____
_____
_____
_____
_____
_____
_____
_____
_____
_____
_____
_____

5. Ephesians 6:5–9

_____
_____
_____
_____
_____
_____
_____
_____
_____
_____
_____
_____
_____
_____

WEEK 6, DAY 3

WORD STUDY NOTES #1

[1] Often, verse 21 is neglected, and we begin this section with verse 22. The instruction for wives would have been seen as commonplace and ordinary in the first century. The real surprise for an ancient reader would have been the call for mutual submission that occurs in verse 21. That short verse immediately placed Paul outside traditional ancient practice. We should not miss this important difference.

[2] A larger surprise is that Paul addresses women directly. Household codes typically only addressed the male head of household, but Paul shows here that he thought women were worthy of address. This was not only different but would have been scandalous in the first century.

90

WORD STUDY NOTES #2

[1] A modern reader always needs to remember the context of biblical passages. It is important to compare how different Paul is when compared to Greek writers of the same era. Aristotle is an excellent example of the prevailing Greek expectations. From his *Politics, Book 1*, he writes, "A husband . . . rules over his wife and children." He further adds, "the courage of a man is shown in commanding, of a woman in obeying." Later he writes, "silence is a woman's glory." This is representative of the content of other household codes. We must keep this background in mind when we read Paul's command to husbands to love their wives. The command to love, which seems so expected in our day, would have been shocking in Paul's time.

What's Happening in the Passage?

As we read through these passages there are certain ideas and words that were familiar to the original readers but are not as familiar to us. Two thousand years and a vastly different culture obscure some of these ideas from us today. You may encounter some of these words and ideas in your study today. Some of them have been explained in more detail in the **Word Study Notes**. If you want even more detail you can supplement this study with a Bible dictionary or commentary.

Create your own brief description of Paul's message in 5:21–24.

1. Ephesians 5:21–24[1,2]

_____

_____

_____

_____

_____

_____

_____

_____

2. Ephesians 5:25–28

Once again, Paul surprises his readers with his command that husbands must love their wives.[1] In Greco-Roman culture the wife was expected to raise honorable children and be a good hostess. The expectation for men was far less restrictive. The male head-of-household was to rule all people in his household, and it was expected that he would find sexual release outside of marriage with whomever he wanted, male or female. If an ancient reader read Paul with the expectation that he would command men to rule their wives, the reader would be disappointed.

3. Ephesians 5:29–33

It is important to note the larger theme that Paul continues in this passage. There is the ongoing call for unity, only now the call is to the husband and wife. If unity between Jew and gentile is a sign to the powers that Jesus is Lord, so it is in the home. Paul has already placed the call for unity in mutual submission. In this passage Paul commands husbands to love their wives and implores wives to respect their husbands. The mutual nature of his instruction contrasts sharply with the larger culture.

Practice the above pattern to summarize the reality that is portrayed in 6:1–4.

4. Ephesians 6:1–4[1]

_____

_____

_____

_____

_____

_____

_____

_____

_____

_____

5. Ephesians 6:5–9

It is important to avoid the political climate when we read these verses.[1] The title "slaves" does not mean what we assume in a North American context. A far closer understanding would be "workers" or "servants." The issue for Paul is not a local political issue, but the larger issue of living in a manner that brings honor and glory to God.

WORD STUDY NOTES #4

[1] We live in a time and culture that is very concerned with the well-being of children. This was not the case when Paul wrote Ephesians. Paul addressing children would have been as surprising as Paul addressing women directly. Children should not be in the background for the Christian but are a vital part of the faith.

WORD STUDY NOTES #5

[1] Slavery in the Roman Empire was a widespread institution that bore little resemblance to the chattel system that flourished in North America in the eighteenth and nineteenth centuries. Roman slavery was a far more widespread practice with almost half the population classified as slaves. Slavery was also spread across a number of jobs. Some slaves were highly paid and honored, serving as physicians or house philosophers. In fact, Plato was himself a slave. Some slaves were able to volunteer to serve as slaves for a fixed period of time, and others were able to buy their own freedom. When we read instructions to slaves in this passage, we should not assume that forced laborers were the readers; the likely readers were probably the average slaves who were paid and who performed a number of household duties. It should also be noted that distinguishing between the ancient Roman system of slavery and the early-American system of slavery is a matter of historical clarification and does not mean that we make excuses for or condone slavery in any form. Christians today should absolutely denounce any type of slavery, whether in the form of free and involuntary labor, or indentured servitude, or in the form of wages that are too low to allow people to earn an independent living.

Discoveries

Let's summarize our discoveries from Ephesians 5:21–6:9.

1. Paul grounds his instruction to husbands and wives in mutual submission.

2. Paul broke the rules of his culture when he directly addressed women in his household code.

3. Slavery in the Roman Empire was a far different practice than the slavery from North American history.

4. Slaves were held in relatively high esteem and were often well paid in the Roman Empire.

5. Paul was not writing to address a political argument in his time but was writing to the church about how they were to live.

WEEK 6, DAY 4

Relationships in the Kingdom and the Story of God

Whenever we read a biblical text, it is important to ask how the particular text we are reading relates to the rest of Scripture. Marriage is important in the Bible. From the creation story where marriage is instituted by God, through Scripture, where the relationship between God and his people is described with marriage imagery, the husband-wife relationship is a foundational element of the Bible.

Places in Scripture where this theme is notably present include but are not limited to Genesis 2:18–25, 29:15–20, 1 Corinthians 7:10–14, and Revelation 21:1–4. **In the space given below, summarize how each passage utilizes the theme of marriage in the kingdom of God.**

Genesis 2:18–25

_____

_____

_____

_____

_____

_____

_____

_____

_____

_____

_____

_____

_____

_____

If you have a study Bible, it may have references in a margin, a middle column, or footnotes that point to other biblical texts. You may find it helpful in understanding how the whole story of God ties together to look up some of those other scriptures from time to time.

93

Genesis 29:15–20

_____

_____

_____

_____

_____

_____

1 Corinthians 7:10–14

_____

_____

_____

_____

_____

_____

_____

_____

_____

_____

Revelation 21:1–4

_____

_____

_____

_____

_____

WEEK 6, DAY 5

Ephesians and Our World Today

When we look at the theme of relationships in the kingdom in Ephesians 5:21–6:9, it can become the lens through which we see ourselves, our world, and how God works in our world today.

1. Why is verse 21 so frequently ignored today, and verse 22 so prominent?

We often let tradition or the politics of our own day influence how we read the Bible. Many

people were raised in or remember a time when women were not granted the same opportunities

as men. So, unfortunately, we might start reading this passage with verse 22 if it fits our

expectations better, and ignore verse 21.

Following the above example, answer these questions about how we can understand ourselves, our world, and God's action in our world today.

2. How does the information about other Greek household codes change how we read this passage?

3. In what ways is this passage still relevant for us today?

4. How do you think many people today misunderstand these verses about slavery?

_____

_____

_____

_____

_____

_____

_____

_____

5. Does the clarification about slavery in the Roman Empire impact your understanding of this passage?

_____

_____

_____

_____

_____

_____

_____

6. Have you ever thought about the importance of unity between husband and wife impacting our larger world?

_____

_____

_____

_____

_____

_____

_____

Invitation and Response

God's Word always invites a response. Think about the way the theme of relationships in the kingdom speaks to us today. How does it invite us to respond?

We are invited to consider how God loves those with whom we are in relationships.

This passage in God's Word gives us the opportunity to outwardly respect and honor

the people in our lives from a place of deep respect and honor for God.

What is your evaluation of yourself based on any or all of the verses found in Ephesians 5:21-6:9?

It is impossible to live a triumphant life if our homes do not bear the marks of Christ.

EPHESIANS 6:10-24

In this concluding section of Ephesians, the temptation is to think that Paul has already said all the important things. We should notice that Paul still has some important things to say. At the close of the letter Paul prepares his troops for the battle that still remains. These are words that are meant to inspire the church and remind them that the enemy is real. The forces that the church fought in Paul's time — and still fights today — are flesh and blood, but are also supernatural. We should never seek to fight this battle using only our own strength.

WEEK 7, DAY 1

Absorb the passage in Ephesians 6:10–24 by reading it aloud several times until you become familiar with its verses, words, and phrases.

WEEK 7, DAY 2

EPHESIANS 6:10-24

The Setting

This is a passage where it is vital to remember what is happening. Paul wrote this letter from prison. He was imprisoned for spreading the gospel and for working tirelessly to fully include the gentiles. He also wrote this in an empire where Nero was emperor. The power imbalance in ancient Rome was incredible. Nero had all of the power, and the Christians had none. The believers did not have economic or social clout; they did not even have a vote. The power in control had the ability to crush every part of the church.

The political powers were easy to see. These early believers struggled not only against these political entities but also against the spiritual forces that supported the efforts of Rome. This was not some fringe belief but was a common conception of the spiritual world. If the believers were to prevail they must prepare diligently, and fight with the ever-present help of the Spirit.

The Message

It is easy to get sidetracked and try to discern the exact identity of the enemies Paul describes. It would be far easier to say that Paul has a comprehensive view of the battle Christians have in this world. We battle rulers and governments—this was especially true in the first century—but we also battle spiritual forces that aid and strengthen the foes of the church.

Paul wants to simply remind the recipients of this letter that their real enemy is never a person but is always the forces that stand behind those who seek their destruction. These forces are not to be fought with only human tactics. Instead, divine power and strength need to be marshaled to overcome their power. Even as we struggle, we are called to remember that we are seated in the heavenly realms with the resurrected Christ, so we need not fear these enemies. We need to depend on divine strength in the battle.

To discover the message of Ephesians 6:10–24, let's divide the passage into four sections. **Summarize or paraphrase the general message or theme of each grouping of verses (following the pattern provided for verses 10–12).**

1. Ephesians 6:10–12

The spiritual battle we face is real. The strength required to fight the enemy comes from the Lord alone, and the armor we wear is provided by God through the Holy Spirit.

_____

_____

_____

2. Ephesians 6:13–15

_____

_____

_____

_____

_____

3. 3. Ephesians 6:16–20

_____

_____

_____

_____

_____

4. Ephesians 6:21–24

_____

_____

_____

_____

_____

WEEK 7, DAY 3

What's Happening in the Passage?

As we read through these passages there are certain ideas and words that were familiar to the original readers but are not as familiar to us. Two thousand years and a vastly different culture obscure some of these ideas from us today. You may encounter some of these words and ideas in your study today. Some of them have been explained in more detail in the **Word Study Notes**. If you want even more detail you can supplement this study with a Bible dictionary or commentary.

1. Ephesians 6:10–12

These words might fit a military leader preparing their troops for battle. It is a reminder that life will not always be easy and there are inevitable struggles ahead. Believers are reminded that their strength does not rest in their own ability but in the Lord, who sits in the heavenly realms. Since we are seated with Christ, believers do not need to fear. We often read these verses as individuals, but this passage is written to the church as a whole. We do not struggle alone against these powers[1] but as a collective people of God.

Create your own brief summary or description of the reality portrayed in verses 13–15.

2. Ephesians 6:13–15[1]

_____

_____

_____

_____

_____

_____

_____

WORD STUDY NOTES #1

[1] People have speculated about the identity of the powers Paul mentions in verse 12. A description of Daniel from the Dead Sea Scrolls sheds some light on Paul's words in Ephesians. This account depicts a spiritual war in which righteous Israel is assisted by angelic forces, and they overwhelm demonic powers under the control of Belial, who is the leader of evil spiritual forces. This imagery of divine warfare with the traditional enemies of Israel and their dark, spiritual helpers provides the best way to understand Paul's language here. We should also note that this is a reference to the demonic powers being defeated, which is clearly Paul's intent in Ephesians as well. Any Christian who fears these demonic forces is missing the point of Ephesians.

WORD STUDY NOTES #2

[1] Paul uses a great deal of imagery in this passage. We should not allow ourselves to be distracted by the visuals of the military armor; instead, we need to look at the qualities Paul espouses. The church should exemplify the qualities of truth, righteousness, peace, and faith. We are instructed to stand firm with these divine qualities. The temptation is always there for believers to retreat before the enemy, which would not fit those who are seated with Christ. We should also not be looking for reasons to attack. While the battle rages around us, the enemy will try to sow seeds of discord. With peace and truth on our side, our only requirement is to stand firm in the face of these attacks.

[1] At the close of this letter Paul uses two contrasting terms to describe himself. He is an "ambassador in chains." An ambassador normally enjoys great privileges in life, but Paul languishes under house arrest. This is how Paul saw his ministry. Instead of complaining about his difficult situation, he understands the potential his life still has. Perhaps this is a reminder to the church to always remember the potential they have in spite of the adversities they may face.

[1] Paul uses a unique word to close the letter, and there is some question about which word it is being used to describe. It is a word that is translated "in immortality." Most versions of the New Testament use it to describe love, as in an undying love. Yet it is possible that it could also be used to describe the grace that flows to believers. Either way it is a fitting end to Paul's letter—a message written to people he does not know but who will experience the love and grace of God for eternity.

3. Ephesians 6:16–20

The helmet of salvation is a reference to Isaiah 59:17, where the Lord puts on the same item. Notice that the church is asked to take the helmet of salvation and put it on. The church has already obtained this salvation, and they must put this salvation to use in their lives. We play an active role in what God wants to do through us.

We might also note the presence of the Spirit in Isaiah 59:21, and how strongly this parallels Paul's description of the Spirit here in Ephesians. This struggle[1] is not alone; it is done with the indwelling presence of the Spirit.

Summarize what Paul is saying in verses 21–24.

4. Ephesians 6:21–24[1]

_____

_____

_____

_____

_____

_____

_____

_____

_____

_____

_____

_____

_____

_____

_____

_____

_____

_____

Discoveries

Let's summarize our discoveries from Ephesians 6:10–24.

1. Paul realizes that believers struggle against more than flesh and blood; they battle spiritual forces as well.

2. Paul also wants his readers to know that these forces have already been defeated.

3. The imagery of a soldier's armor was not new; it is a reference to the Old Testament. This reference links the armor to the presence of the Holy Spirit, who is our real defense.

4. Even though Paul is in prison, he sees his ministry as being an ambassador. Our earthly circumstances never dictate our true effectiveness.

5. We have reason to hope because the grace and love of Christ will be experienced in eternity for those who place their hope in Christ.

Eternity and the Story of God

Whenever we read a biblical text, it is important to ask how the particular text we are reading relates to the rest of Scripture. In these concluding words of Ephesians, Paul hints at the eternal nature of our life in Christ. There are many other places in the New Testament that share this important promise. Explore these other passages and determine if there is a consistent theme among them.

Places in Scripture where this theme is notably present include but are not limited to John 3:16, 1 Corinthians 15:42–44, 1 Thessalonians 4:16–18, 1 Peter 1:3–5, and 1 John 5:10–12. **In the space given below, summarize how each passage utilizes the theme of eternity with Christ.**

John 3:16

_____

_____

_____

_____

_____

_____

1 Corinthians 15:42–44

_____

_____

_____

_____

_____

_____

_____

_____

If you have a study Bible, it may have references in a margin, a middle column, or footnotes that point to other biblical texts. You may find it helpful in understanding how the whole story of God ties together to look up some of those other scriptures from time to time.

1 Thessalonians 4:16-18

1 Peter 1:3-5

1 John 5:10-12

WEEK 7, DAY 5

Ephesians and Our World Today

When we look at the theme of fighting the battle with eternity in mind in Ephesians 6:10–24, it can become the lens through which we see ourselves, our world, and how God works in our world today.

1. Do Christians typically fight with God's strength, or do we try to go it alone?

As much as we agree with the idea of fighting with God's strength, we often try to engage our

battles in our own strength. We forget that our own reasoning and determination are futile

compared to the spiritual power God makes available to us.

_____

Following the above example, answer these questions about how we can understand ourselves, our world, and God's action in our world today.

2. In what ways do we fight spiritual powers, and how does Christ help us?

_____

_____

_____

_____

_____

_____

3. Why does Paul have to remind believers to stand firm with peace?

_____

_____

_____

_____

_____

_____

4. How could Paul be an ambassador from prison?

_____

_____

_____

_____

_____

_____

_____

_____

_____

_____

_____

_____

_____

5. In what ways do we allow circumstances to determine our view of ourselves in Christ?

_____

_____

_____

_____

_____

_____

_____

_____

_____

_____

_____

_____

_____

Invitation and Response

God's Word always invites a response. Think about the way the theme of fighting the battle with eternity in mind speaks to us today. How does it invite us to respond?

Paul's closing words in Ephesians invite us to keep our eyes on God as we navigate the

spiritual battles in life. We can put on the armor he gives us and fight the battle with

cconfidence, resting in the security God provides through Christ now and for eternity.

What is your evaluation of yourself based on any or all of the verses found in Ephesians 6:10–24?

*We have reason to hope because
the grace and love of Christ will be
experienced in eternity for those
who place their hope in Christ.*